The Dummies' Guide to Software Testing

K Venkatanarasiman

First Edition

© 2018, K Venkatanarasiman

ISBN: 9781718179745

This page is left blank intentionally.

CONTENTS

Preface   v

What's inside? ix

Chapter 1: What is the need for Software Testing? 1

Chapter 2: What it Takes to become a Software
            Tester   8

Chapter 3: A tester's typical work profile   22

Chapter 4: Learning; Investing in the right place 25

Chapter 5: Testing Job Search tips   34

Chapter 6: Factors to consider for a testing role 41

Chapter 7: Software development Life Cycle,
            Software Testing Life Cycle, and Basic
            Testing Techniques   47

Chapter 8: Test Management Tools and
            Automation Tools   71

Chapter 9: Recent Trends   75

Chapter 10: Testing Resources   92

Concluding Remarks   100

Acronyms and Abbreviations   101

This page is left blank intentionally.

PREFACE

Hello Reader,

Thank you for your interest in this book. I have been serving as an independent QA Consultant for over a decade now. Most of the topics discussed in this book are a true reflection of the experiences. The ideas presented are central to anyone aspiring or starting a career in software testing.

I have played active roles in Quality Assurance and Project Management, primarily in Medical device product development. I have interacted with various cultures through significant International Client-Facing engagements.

My expertise is in handling complex projects involving Verification and Validation. I have collaborated with many leading US-based Medical Device Companies. Currently, I work for a niche Medical device startup.

I'm equipped with a meritorious MBA, pursued jointly at the University of Bradford, UK and University of Perugia, Italy. The B-school is FT ranked and among the top elite 58 "Triple Accredited" Bschools in the world. I also have a good exposure to STEM fields and engineering. I have a distinction in Bachelor of Engineering (BE) in Electrical and Electronics at Annamalai University, India. I also pursued Master of Science (MS) in Software Systems, at BITS Pilani, India. These effectively complement my B-School erudition. My early schooling and Junior College education were in Bangalore, India.

The day I logged my first defect was a proud moment. I thought I did make a positive impact on patient or end user experience. After exposure to various phases of product development, I reflect on my learning. Mistakes were sometimes part of the learning curve, but the lessons were inspiring. Now I'm not only a software tester but also a Medical device product development consultant.

My motivation for this book is to serve as a beginner's guide for aspiring and budding software testers. The aim is to help the prospective tester establish a meaningful career path. I'm a believer in providing concise information for creating an enhanced reading experience. I have taken every effort to keep each of the chapters crisp and to the point.

This book is a tip of the iceberg and not a bible of concepts which would suit every context. There are plenty of books on core testing concepts and Software engineering as a whole. This is probably not one of them. However, it is a good starting point for digging deeper in the software testing space. There are a variety of resources for selection based on the area of interest.

This book influences my interactions with industry leaders, testing forums, customers, and end-users. Cross-functional teams, developers, regulatory personnel, project managers and business directors also provided insights.

I would be delighted to get your feedback on topics which I may not have touched upon.

K Venkatanarasiman

ΛΛΛ

K Venkatanarasiman

This page is left blank intentionally.

WHAT'S INSIDE?

Chapter 1: What is the need for Software Testing?

This chapter deals with the need for Software testing for a project which impacts businesses and services aligned towards product development.

Chapter 2: What it Takes to become a Software Tester

This chapter deals with the traits required for you to become a successful Software Tester.

Chapter 3: A tester's typical work profile

A day in the life of a tester can be repetitive but unique to each project. This chapter draws the learnings from the previous chapters and uses it to sketch the typical day to day work in the life of a software tester.

Chapter 4: The Learning; Investing in the right place

This chapter explores the various resources available, possible traps to avoid and the worthy learning suggestions.

Chapter 5: Testing Job Search tips

This chapter introduces you to some basic traps that a prospective tester falls prey to, during the job search phase. It recommends some basic tips to showcase yourself in a resume followed by the interview process.

Chapter 6: Factors to consider for a testing role

Quality is the bigger picture. Testing is a subset which as several layers and flavors to it based on the project needs. This chapter dwells on exploring some of the factors to consider while you take up a testing role.

Chapter 7: Software development Life Cycle, Software Testing Life Cycle, and Basic Testing Techniques

This chapter refers to some of the key testing concepts taken from the testing literature and provides you with a basic understanding of the knowledge base needed for a Software Tester. This chapter is not very extensive in theory but serves well to equip the tester with the know-how.

Chapter 8: Test Management Tools and Automation Tools

The testing life cycle may get cumbersome in handling the processes and volume of documentation depending on the size and complexity of the testing project. This chapter explores few of the options available to you as a tester to perform your task efficiently using the right tool.

Chapter 9: Recent Trends

It is very important for the modern tester to stay relevant in the current industry. This chapter dwells upon such key areas.

Chapter 10: Testing Resources

This chapter contains a collection of useful testing resources handpicked by a community of testers. This will take you a long way on the journey to a Subject Matter Expert.

ΔΔΔ

CHAPTER 1

WHAT IS THE NEED FOR SOFTWARE TESTING?

Software testing is a process of executing the test system with the intent of finding software anomalies. It can also be stated as the process of validating and verifying that the software under test meets the business, technical and regulatory requirements.

This chapter deals with the need for Software testing for a project which impacts businesses and services aligned towards product development.

When considering the various arguments for implementing adequate Quality Assurance (QA) and Testing processes, none is more convincing than the costs associated with fixing defects. The longer a defect goes undetected, the costlier it is to fix. Simple costs vs benefits analysis will overwhelmingly exhibit that the benefits of employing a QA Test Engineer to verify and validate the System/Unit far outweigh the costs.

Software testing should be done to find errors in the code, the interface, the design, etc. as early as possible in the process. The later you find a problem, the more it costs to fix due to increased complexity. Apply Pareto's principle - roughly 80% of the effects come from 20% of the causes. So, it is wise to brainstorm, identify and mitigate the 20% as early as possible in the development lifecycle.

Project Management 101 emphasizes three critical items – **Cost**, **Quality** and **Time**. Let's analyze Cost versus Time. If you find a defect during development, the cost is developer rework and re-running basic tests. But during documentation, the code, the tests, and the documentation need updates in addition to defect log on how the problem was fixed. This is at least three times the cost of finding it in development. From there, the costs skyrocket exponentially. The worst scenario of all is for a customer or an end user to find the defect. That's going to cost you lots to fix, plus it could cost you the customer itself. It could even land the company in a lawsuit.

You might want to think about 'COPQ' - the Cost of Poor Quality. This is an analysis typically done in manufacturing. It looks at all the costs to the business of mistakes, errors, and failures both in the production process and out in the marketplace. Breaking COPQ down into each of the various costs and doing a simple analysis of what they add up to can be eye-opening! Then you need to assess the quality impact that your improvements might make, to demonstrate the savings that could result.

Q: When does testing need to be done?

A: At just about every major point in your development lifecycle.

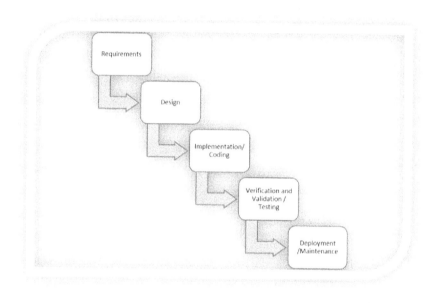

Figure 1. A Classic Water fall Model in SDLC

It requires the tester to think like an end user or customer instead of the developer. The basic testing, automated suites and such, have to be comprehensive enough to cause a high level of belief the product meets its intended use. That, though, is less than half the testing. The other half is exploratory testing, where the tester literally "plays" with the system. This phase of the testing can look like the tester is just playing around. Sometimes they are. Usually, though, they are trying things that only an end user would do. The best approach to exploratory testing is to develop personalities to play while testing. (New user, experienced user, service user, administrator etc.)

Figure 2 Terminologies that you would encounter

Q: Who should do the testing?

A: A person who has skills in finding, documenting and reporting defects, in debugging, in understanding and being able to explain the difference between design, requirements, intended use, and actual implementation.

If your project doesn't deploy independent testers, you should at least have someone other than the development team who performs testing. A developer testing their own code is mandatory, but it will only find the more obvious bugs that you think are bugs and are limited to a module or unit. Testing one's own module or sub-system can be much like having one accountable for being one's own lawyer. It doesn't work out all the time.

What makes QA and testing important though is more than the above points: it's about building a positive reputation for developing quality products. Any upscaling business shall be willing to pay more for high quality, safe and reliable products, and therefore QA and testing could contribute a great deal of value. By being able to reassure the customer that everything possible is being accomplished to ensure a high-quality product meeting the defined requirements, you can increase your customer's confidence that the project will be completed on schedule and within budget.

The role of the QA Test Engineer is essential to these aims because developer self-testing is unreliable and a clear conflict of interest. The independence and impartiality of the QA Test Engineer must be beyond question, proving independence is key to reassuring the project outcome.

The Long-term acid test for an effective QA testing is **customer satisfaction**: are your clients jumping ship (looking elsewhere), or do they have increased confidence in your work? Projects completed late or not at all and going well beyond the allocated budget, regulatory fines, product recalls are classic outcomes of a QA & testing failure.

Compliance with industry-specific software standards is often a prerequisite to being able to bid for and win business. The purpose of Software Quality Assurance (SQA) is to ensure that software engineering processes used throughout all phases of development are the correct ones for the associated industry standards such as ISO9000, CMMI (maturity model) or Automotive SPICE to name just a few examples. Some domains such as Medical devices and Aeronautics are highly regulated and have regulatory standards such as ISO13485 and DO-178 in addition to quality and risk management standards. There are also regulatory bodies such as FDA and FAA for US-based regulated products. This is essential in safety-critical industries where malfunctioning devices can potentially cause serious injury or even the loss of human life. An organization's QMS (Quality Management System) should be built on these standards and regulations and should cover all aspects and not limited to Software testing.

This chapter set the scene for software testing. It threw light on the need for software testing by considering the Cost of poor quality and also who should perform testing. The next chapter shall use this information and explore the traits needed for you to become a software tester.

ΔΛΔ

CHAPTER 2

WHAT IT TAKES TO BECOME A SOFTWARE TESTER

Software Testing is not rocket science but it requires you to *think outside the box*. Testing scenarios, in general, are idea-oriented but reporting them may be process oriented.

This chapter deals with the traits required for you to become a successful Software Tester.

Q: Is it necessary to have an IT background to be a software tester?

A: What exactly is an 'IT Background'? A degree in Computer Science? Work experience in the IT industry? In my honest opinion, a background in IT is not mandatory to be a software tester (or a developer). You can learn these skills on your own. You just need a computer, internet connectivity, the test artifact, some logical thinking abilities, and lots of patience.

Getting your first job without an IT background can be hard. You need to figure out ways to get noticed by employers, and secure interviews and make your opportunities count.

Actual role and pay depends on a lot of factors such as

- Work Experience
- Years of job-related experience in the domain or industry
- Communication – Both written and verbal. Ability to create and maintain technical, business or project documents. Ability to take notes of facts and meeting minutes.
- Exposure to the domain
- Exposure to the industry
- Exposure to the processes
- Ability to work with cross-functional teams
- Commitment to up-scale your learning continuously
- Your target companies and what company/pay scale you are at currently.
- Your flexibility to invest time as an employee, contractor or a consultant.
- Most importantly, your disruptive X-factor that can contribute to the business outcomes

Q: What about the pay grade?

A: In general, a tester's average pay can range ± 15% of a developer's pay. This is just a rough estimate and not based on any standard rule. Industry related median salary for a testing role could be found using reputable sources such as Glassdoor or LinkedIn Salary. You may equate the same for per hour pay rate for contractor or consultant roles.

You may think that the developers test the code themselves questioning the need for a quality assurance team. In this highly competitive technological world, most projects are complex. Hence there is a need for a team that can ensure that the software product meets the intended requirements and does not crash when the end user uses it.

The QA team shall identify the areas which result in a scrap which do not meet the intended requirements or product specifications. The result could impact revenue savings. Early identification of defects in the production process decreases the cost of repairing them. If these defects are found at the end of the production process they will be costlier to fix and if found by the client it will convey a very negative impression of the company and product standards.

Suggested Reading: *5 Most Embarrassing Software Bugs in History*

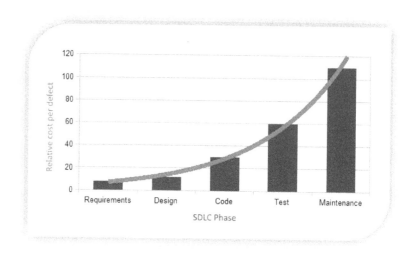

Figure 3 Cost of Quality

Ultimately, Customer satisfaction and brand loyalty increase when the elimination of defective products. Hence, there should be a constant evaluation of the process to improve products and services.

An organization having a QA team is more likely to be confident about their work and can be better equipped to gain customer satisfaction. The QA team actively seeks methods for continuous improvement so that services which are not offered by their companies are provided. QA helps the workforce of a company to develop a competitive niche in the industry.

In smaller companies, the number of inspections by the QA team in software development is reduced. They effectively use the developers time spent on evaluating the system. There is an acceptable amount of risk involved in this approach which is to be identified and mitigated in the Risk Management process.

The customer reviews and comments are really crucial and beneficial to determine the QA team efficiency.

CAREER GROWTH IN SOFTWARE TESTING

It is not unusual for testing to yield negative results at product inception. Testing is an iterative and evolving process targeting constant improvement, starting from some level of incompetence and slowly moving towards 100% conformance. This testing cycle repeats itself with the release of every new product!

Career growth in software testing has little to do with your ability to test or to script automation code. It has to do with your ability to make yourself and the team unearth, document, fix and archive all the defects. That comes down to doing a good risk assessment. You have to develop a feel for where the defects will be and how to surface them, and how to report them in a way that gets results. It may be that you should convince a developer to make a particular obscure segment of functionality more testable. It may be convincing a teammate to pair test with you to double-check your work. It may be creating an automated framework to load the system until it breaks. By exercising good judgment in the use of your time and others', arguing persuasively for practices that effectively reduce product risk, and showing leadership in caring about quality, you should advance your career positively. If you feel stuck, then start setting up and interacting with a network of testers whom you respect and demonstrate your worth to them. Test team leadership and senior management are good leadership paths further along in your career.

Through my career I learned different traits to achieve career growth, here are some of the key tips that would help you how to improve career growth.

Pick a Path

You can take a few paths in testing. Manual testing is the most well-known part in QA and is a good starting point. This can be a good compensating task if you have a characteristic interest and appreciate in adapting to new products or systems.

To move up in the QA organization after a few years of manual testing, you can choose to take a technical path or a test management path. With a little effort and investment, you can transition to a design engineer, project manager, Agile Scrum Master, Regulatory specialist or a Business analyst.

If you prefer testing and you have a talent for coding and scripting, consider learning 'test automation' as well as 'security testing'. In the event that you choose a technical path, you should keep abreast with the latest technologies. If you are testing websites, User interfaces or Mobile apps there are a lot of tools available for screen recording and playback. This can be the good starting point for automation.

Then again, if you like driving a group and persuading individuals to give a valiant effort, consider being a Test Lead or Test Manager. In the event that you are a Talented QA Manager, you can climb the organization ladder to a Senior Manager, Director or Senior Director. With the expanding repute of Testing Centers of Excellence (TCoE), more QA official positions are opening up at the VP and SVP levels. Senior-level positions regularly require propelled degrees like an MBA or an MIS degree.

Entrepreneurship is also an attractive option, should it interest you. New product startups and consulting companies are emerging more prominently than ever.

Be professional

With pure luck and organizational politics apart, the greatest distinction between the person who advances in the corporate ladder and the person who stays at a similar level forever is the capacity to communicate effectively and coexist with others. Negative practices like whimpering and griping and scrutinizing others can negatively impact progress.

One of the most important traits of a QA professional is integrity and documenting the facts. Keep in mind the end goal to be viewed as a trusted guide it is imperative frankly, reliable and straightforward. Managing by facts and reliable measurements instead of feelings and assessments is the right way of offering intrinsic benefit and acquiring trust.

Take up challenging projects

To develop progressively, look at testing ventures outside the usual range of familiarity. I review the first occasion when I was made a request to set up an independent QA group at Off-shore. Subsequent to setting up an offshore team, I picked up a more prominence for the upsides and downsides of driving a complex medical device V&V project. I took in a considerable measure and picked up certainty by accomplishing something that I hadn't done recently. So, I generally suggest volunteering for demonstrating leadership or innovation whenever possible.

Be Proactive

In an ideal world, you may be accessible to administrators or tutors that will appreciate you and help you along, and that is awesome. In any case, do not hold up until the point when your administrator requests that you train on another expertise or take an additional class. Proactively request your organization to provide resources for enhancing and development.

Also put in the effort and resources in the event your organization's Knowledge Management is inadequate, to bridge any gaps. Join a QA affiliation group, participate in testing meet-ups, read books and articles and apply to talk at gatherings. Affirmations are profitable at a very early stage in your inclination to learn QA basics. Most importantly, do not wait for your supervisor to assign the next task to you, rather suggest the next move.

Own your career growth

In case that you have hit a block in your progression, it might be an ideal opportunity to look for other options. In innovation-centric professions, you may need to switch jobs at some point for continuous growth. For a few people, filling in as a temporary worker or specialist is an ideal approach to get industrywide exposures. A word of caution here: If you repeatedly switch jobs, imminent businesses may scrutinize your commitment. Hence, you should discover a fine balance between switching roles and sustaining at a workplace for an elongated amount of time. At the same time, you should show the security and commitment that organizations look for.

Put the customer first

Businesses continuously adjust the requirements from time to time based on the market needs. The agenda behind entrepreneurs and business directors often conflicting, particularly on a basic programming venture. You should adapt to the customer's needs and be flexible, however, as a value addition you can identify and suggest any gaps.

Avoid these traps at all costs:

These traps can be negatively contributing factors in your testing mission:

- Missing vital bugs regularly during sprints.
- Not being able to provide detailed reports and failure to communicate clearly to other team members, customers, developers about what issues are.
- Little interest in the job, and no developing of skills.
- Not having curiosity or an inquisitive mindset or the inclination to develop domain knowledge for the software that is being tested.
- Failure to master the necessary tools/technical skills needed to do the job, and no interest in developing same.
- Not being able to learn from mistakes made on the job.

If you are a junior tester, focus on documenting test cases and expected results for regression testing. Try to imaging use cases that the senior tester may have missed. Inside of every entry-level tester is a senior tester trying to get out. Try to research methods of partially automating regression testing to facilitate continual deployment.

Be in the end user's shoes

Your activity is to see the product or system from the point of view of the end user and utilize your preparation and aptitude to find anomalies.

Q: *Is it imperative to consider the contribution of key partners?*

A: *Completely. In any case, genuine testing experts ought to dependably keep the client best informed and be a supporter of their ideal experience.*

Focus on Technical Elements, Process and Domain

Software testing is a three-dimensional activity.

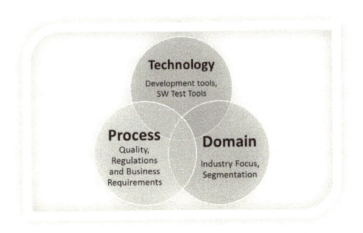

Figure 4 Testing dimensions

On one side you work with niche tools in the industry such as SQL, selenium, Java, QTP etc. On the other side, you are also involved in gathering domain knowledge like working for a finance, bank, retail, Telecom or any other domain and lastly, you have the quality processes, standards, and regulations. Being an entry-level tester, you should focus on all the three aspects. You could choose to specialize in any one dimension later on for career development.

If you chose to grow in technical aspects, you may start upskilling with test automation tools like Selenium, QTP, Soap UI, JMeter etc. The current demand of the industry is to minimize human effort by automating the manual redundant test execution processes. Also, you may choose to acquire knowledge of other testing tools which are widely used in the industry now.

For Test Management, reporting and defect tracking there are various tools like HP ALM, JIRA, Clear Quest etc. Then we have tools like DOORS, Rational Clear Case etc. which provides end to end Requirements management. Once you are familiar, you could use this exposure in performing a role such as a test lead or test manager. Such roles require technical expertise required for testing.

It is also a very good option if you chose to specialize in your domain. I will try to explain this with two examples:

> Suppose you are working for a particular bank and you are aware of all the process and work-flows of the bank; you could equip to become a *banking domain test expert.*

> Suppose there is a tool in the market for calculating the agent's commission in the insurance domain and you are hands-on with that tool, you could equip to become a *banking domain test expert.*

These days, product-based companies are happy to hire domain testing experts. For example, a tester working in bank domain is of little use to a telecom company's vision.

In domains such as an ERP, it is even possible to completely transform your profile from tester to a functional expert if you demonstrate good domain knowledge.

Lastly, the Process is also closely tied to the domain and any additional knowledge on quality standards, regulations, GMP and GDP standards are very valuable for a tester. It is possible to transform your profile from tester to a QA auditor or a regulatory specialist if you choose to specialize in this track.

It is also not uncommon to see some testers to apply themselves, learn to code, and become engineers on the product while others move into management. In the end, it all depends on what you are testing, but most manual testers have some knowledge of networking and how computers work. They also need to have a good attention to detail. A good tester should quickly gain familiarity with the product they are testing and find an area of focus that is best suited for career progression.

This chapter went on to explain the required traits for software testing. It summarized the background needed, the possible earnings, possible career paths and the qualities that help you become a successful software tester. The next chapter shall use this information and dig deeper to explore the work profile and a typical workday in the life of a tester.

ΔΔΔ

CHAPTER 3

A TESTER'S TYPICAL WORK PROFILE

A day in the life of a tester can be repetitive but unique to each project. This chapter draws the learnings from the previous chapters and uses it to sketch the typical day to day work in the life of a software tester.

It typically starts with you being assigned to a project that involves software testing. The First task to do upon assignment is to read the documents to understand the product or the system. This would involve brainstorming Requirements at various levels: Business, Product, Design, Sub-System, Software, and Standards. Also, try to understand the Software Test Life-cycle (discussed in detail in Chapter 7) and the test plan.

If a mentor is allocated, you may be trained in the organization's QMS and testing process, Defect management tools, Configuration Management tools, Requirements Management, test case management tools, etc. but owing to schedule constraints, sometimes you may not be assigned a mentor, you may have to learn on your own.

After the initial understanding, you may be asked to perform a test design for the requirements you have analyzed. After getting an agreement with stakeholders, you may then expand these test designs to test cases.

Suggested Reading: *Business Requirement Analysis*

Your test cases will likely be reviewed by your mentor or peer or a panel of domain experts to iron out any issues. You will have to update your test cases based on the review comments and get the test cases approved for execution.

You may be assigned a module and be asked to execute the test based on your test case. If you encounter defects, you may raise defects in the defect tracking system.

You may be proud of your first defect but your defects will likely be reviewed by your Peer/Mentor/Lead. If your defect description is clear and complete, it will be assigned to a developer or else you will be asked to update the defect.

It is likely that your organization measures the performance outcomes in every step of this process. Key quality metrics monitored are Defect Removal

Efficiency (DRE) and defect leakage across phases. Hence if you miss defects, you may be scrutinized. Sometimes in a regulated domain, you may have to update a Corrective Action and Preventive Action Document commonly known as CAPA.

Suggested Reading: _Defect management and its advantages_

Once your defect is fixed, you will be asked to perform regression testing. The goal is to verify if the defect is fixed and it does not impact any other modules in the system.

Sometimes you will be asked to verify defects raised by others. The other team member might feel offended because you are verifying their defects. But it is a good practice to verify defects raised by others from the organization's process standpoint.

This entire cycle continues many times over depending on your Product life cycle and the Software Development Life Cycle. More on this in Chapter 7.

This chapter went on to explain the typical day to day work in the life of a software tester. It summarized the tasks to perform after project assignation, the tests you would execute and defect logging. The next chapter shall explore the learning investments that may be needed for a successful testing career.

ΛΛΛ

CHAPTER 4

THE LEARNING; INVESTING IN THE RIGHT PLACE

Continuous learning is very beneficial in all skill areas and software testing is no different. While a lot of learning can be done 'on the job', there are a lot of things you can better achieve if you invest in additional learning. But it is also beneficial if you do it form the right place that gives you the 'value' for this investment.

This chapter explores the various resources available, possible traps to avoid and the worthy learning suggestions.

There are various certifications, scholarly articles, talks, conferences, and resources over the print media and internet that empower you to continuously learn and up-scale. Certifications are the obvious eye-catchers, but sometimes can be money traps economically. This Chapter explains the obvious Myths and provides some useful guidance for further learning.

TESTING MYTH'S

Here is some myth's addressing pro-certification arguments:

- *Myth 1: You have nothing to show on a resume if you're fresher.*

-Not true. You have tons of options for learning and showcasing. Read on.

- *Myth 2: HR and recruiters don't find your resume powerful.*

-Chances are that there are 1,000 of resumes just like yours what makes you think that they will choose you? No general test certification will save a dull resume and compensate for poor interview skills.

- *Myth 3: You'll be able to understand some fundamentals of testing and also know about the standards that are followed in testing.*

-Now ask yourself. Will having read the laws of cricket grant you fundamentals of actually playing the sport? Only to an extent.

- *Myths 4: You'll test your skills in an exam.*

-Memorizing answers to multiple choice questions is not a testing skill. Testing is about asking questions.

- *Myth 5: We could make good use of the certificate as a filter when we have many candidates.*

-I see that's hiring manager speaking. But, such a statement makes you sound lame and lazy! The interview is a two-way road. Is this the main trait you want to showcase?

- *Myth 6: Besides, if you have many candidates, you probably want to choose the best. As we established, certification is a sign of commodity; how will it help you to find a best talent and performer? Having a certification will not harm.*

-If you're paying your own money it may not be a worthy investment. You could choose a real and practical testing training instead. If your employer is paying - watch out: your role is being treated as a commodity. Next step is to replace it with the cheapest bid.

- *Myth 7: If you are interviewed by a non-technical person certification will make a difference.*

-If the interviewer is a "non-technical person" how they're supposed to evaluate technical definitions from the curriculum? If anything, your interpersonal skills will help you to make a difference.

- *Myth 8: It gives you some confidence, before getting a candidate in for an interview, that they at least have some basic knowledge and will know the standard testing terminology.*

- Years of experience in the resume isn't good as a proof of "basic knowledge" and certification logo is? Besides, there's no "standard testing terminology". Each company is free to use their own definitions and so they do. Even with such fundamental entities as "bug", "test case", "severity".

- *Myth 9: It is an industry standard certification accepted across the world, it will give you an edge over others when all are even at their interview.*

- Large players do not recognize testing certifications. They're certification negative.

Suggested Reading: *Are IT certifications worth it?*

- *Myth 10: Certifications help us expand our knowledge base beyond that of our everyday tasks.*

-Learning is what helps us expand our knowledge. Read blogs, read books, participate in tech meetups and conferences. Practice and think about testing. Certifications are a very poor substitute for learning.

- *Myth 11: Certification teaches the standardized testing process.*

-There is no such thing as "standardized testing process" simply because there's no standardized development process.

- *Myth 12: Learning - practically, through exercises - what are the common techniques will help you much better. Which certification or certification training offers real hands-on training in testing techniques? There are few highest paying sectors where ISTQB is a prerequisite (Banking companies, e-commerce, etc.).*

-The statement is debatable and here is my critical analysis:

First, even the proponents of certifications agree that it matters most for getting an entry-level position. Such jobs are not "highest paying" regardless of the sector.

Second, it's not a universal truth that banks or financial companies offer the highest market rate for testing jobs. In fact, I know plenty of examples when the rate offered was below the market average.

Third, it's not a universal truth that having a certification is a "prerequisite". They may be "nice to have" but won't largely matter when compared to the experience and skills.

TESTING SKILLS TO SHOWCASE YOURSELF

I would suggest that a tester or a prospective tester focus on attaining skill-based training. Among the most practical, affordable, available - and valuable, I suggest Cem Kaner's Black Box Software Testing courses. AST offers it online: AST-BBST Courses. As a bonus, you'll make acquaintances in the testing community! Here are some of the focus areas. Later in this book, Chapter 10 provides you with the resources to accomplish many of the points listed below.

- Join Software Testing Club
- Join the Association for Software Testing
- Attend international testing conferences and local testing meetups
- Read testing blogs
- Read books! We have a lot of great books in the industry, pointing to just a few -
- Domain Testing Workbook by Cem Kaner and co-authors
- Explore It! by Elisabeth Hendrickson
- Web Testing Basics - How to Test A Website by Rob Lambert
- Go strategic! Testing is a hands-on activity, but it has much more to it than just pounding a keyboard. Read Gerald Weinberg's book Perfect Software and Other Illusions About Testing. I guarantee it'll become your handbook on testing strategy.
- Create what you consume!

- THINK about what you read and learn. WRITE IT DOWN.
- Better still use mind-maps. They can present a pictorial representation that is easier to remember.
- Start a journal of your learning experiences.
- Start a blog, share your ideas publicly.
- Engage in testing meetups and present yourself.
- PRACTICE. The U-Test platform provides you with demo testing projects.
- Participate in testing challenges.

There's a movement dedicated to software testing craftsmanship. Professionals and newbies around the globe gather for Weekend Testing practice - to learn new skills and share experiences. Look up the nearest (by time zone) chapter and Skype in! It is now on Twitter as well.

GO BEYOND TESTING

- A critical aspect would be to attain people skills
- Not specific to testing but absolutely recommended: master the job search process, from resume writing to the creation of professional digital identity, from interviewed to interviewing others.

BECOME A SUBJECT MATTER EXPERT

An expert is one who could apply knowledge, skill, and experiences to accomplish something effectively and efficiently and at the same time, able to help other people to understand as well.

Below are what I personally understand about the learning level.

1. Know -> Understand -> Practice -> Teach

2. Information -> Knowledge -> Skill/Experience -> Expert

For Software Quality, first, you would need to know about how the quality works and need to know how to do Software Testing so you have relevant information. You then understand apply to the task. Once you get hands on, you gain skill and experience and you would handle any challenges or complexities. This distinguishes you from being a rookie tester and is categorized as an experienced Senior Software Tester.

Lastly, if you are able to spread the knowledge to the community, this is a great leadership trait for being an expert. The more you teach, the more you know.

You may not need much training because you can be self-learner but you indeed need time to practice several times over to build up skills and experiences to become the EXPERT.

This chapter went on to explain the myths and traps a software tester would face in learning investment decision and also suggest the possible and economically viable learning resources to become a testing champion. The next chapter shall explore the job market and suggest job search tips that may be needed for the testing job market.

ΔΔΔ

CHAPTER 5

TESTING JOB SEARCH TIPS

Job search in this economic scenario and competition can get daunting, if not done using a structured approach. Hence you should eliminate as many mistakes as possible and prepare well.

This chapter introduces you to some basic traps that a prospective tester falls prey to, during the job search phase. It recommends some basic tips to showcase yourself in a resume followed by the interview process.

If you feel Interview calls are few and far between, I can foresee three major reasons why this may be happening:

- You get stuck in one skill set and it's time to master new methods, tools, and frameworks.
- Your CV is weak, despite a strong work experience. Maybe, you just need to improve the resume.
- The lack of professional experience doesn't let you showcase all your possibilities. Note that

the lack of experience is not the same as the lack of skills, it's different.

So, here's what you do to address these gaps:

Master new skills in software testing

Even if your CV gets rejected for reasons other than lack of the skills, still read this part. Now, manual testing is hybrid so while working on your skills, have that in mind. Implement testing tools for your work process and learn development. Don't forget to list it on your CV - we are just getting to this point.

Review your Resume

Don't just focus on the fact that you have great manual testing skills. List down all the additional skills you have in automation and development. If you have an experience of cooperation with the marketing team or Regulatory team write that down as well. Now testing teams like to hire developers with a deep understanding of the business process. Marketing and testing are linked strongly, and to have at least the basic understanding of the business strategy is essential.

Suggested Reading: *How to Write a Résumé That Stands Out*

Get your experience you are after

No matter how great your skills are, you also have to possess a strong portfolio and considerable work experience. Sometimes people just don't hire you at some period of time because of your age, or even the way you look, or just because they haven't liked you personally. To overcome such a situation, you may create your own project, partner with a developer and offer free testing, or even better, develop it yourself. Even if it's not going to make to your portfolio, after all, you will boost your skills tremendously.

Also, take a look at the guidelines for gathering a manual testing team. It's important to understand what's going on the other side of the table, in minds of people who are hiring you. A colleague of mine recently asked me, "Where should I start with for preparation of interview? It's almost 2 years I have faced any interview."

WHAT DOES IT TAKE TO MAKE THE CUT?

My answer was straightforward and it applies to both freshers and experienced professionals.

Firstly, know your Testing Concepts: One needs to be very good at this especially the manual testing methodologies. But only knowing different testing concepts is half work done.

The next – most important thing is to know which type/technique/concept of testing can be applied at what stage of SDLC. "What should I test and when" is very important. There might be some concepts, which are not applicable to what we, professional test in our company, but it's always better to have an idea of all testing practices. Chapter 7 explains some of the key testing concepts.

Many freshers and working testing professionals might not have exposure to various testing domains such as localization testing, multilingual testing, time zone testing etc. But knowing more than what you have worked on, will help you better answer the different questions from the interviewer.

I always try to keep my testing knowledge updated above and beyond my current assignment. This can help you a lot while job switches. Consider an interviewer asks you a question on the topic, which you have never worked on. For example, say you don't have any experience on web-based projects or client-server testing and the interviewer asks you to test "Outlook mail application". Will you be able to answer this question? You can. Even if you do not have such exposure previously. How? Curiosity is your friend. So, broaden your thinking area, be curious in every work and every query you face in your daily work routine.

Knowing more is harmless and will definitely help you at least to give your thoughts on the questions asked by the interviewer.

If you don't know any testing concept, e.g. "Localization testing", then try to learn them first. Like – what would be localization testing? It's simple; Test if the application looks local for you while using. Then go on exploring. See for used colors, content, images, culture etc., Different countries, locales have it in a different way. Consider a website that reads from right to left, is it accepted in countries other than the Middle-East? Obviously, NO. Or can you display the same geo-specific content in Japan what you can display in the US? Again NO. This is just a simple example of how you can learn unknown testing concepts.

Lastly, do not be hesitant and be honest with your response.

DIVERSIFYING FROM A TESTING FIELD:

One of the biggest issues I see in the industry is the fact, that very often testers/QAs are not seen on par or as appreciated as the developers and architects, as they are not producing production code. Testing is often viewed as a non-value addition. Additionally, I have been observing how testers have got into their work routine, stop ideating and investing in their learning curve, thinking there is nothing more interesting in the testing area. It is easier for a tester to burnout running after software quality, and if they don't see this transform into a business success story, they can become frustrated. Of course, the general rule for the tester is not to stay too long in one assignment and change from time to time, to leave the comfort zone.

If you are already a Test Manager, you may already know how to test, manage the project and resources. You might have already mastered the Domain. These factors may or may not relevant to the new career that you are looking for.

The following options may be noteworthy:

Other roles within the Industry - Even you start with Software Testing, if you demonstrate your capability you could transform to roles such as Software Developer, Business Analyst, System Architecture, Data Admin at management level or any position relevant. Or you could even start your own Testing Services Company!

Other roles outside the Industry - If you have enough domain knowledge you could change your career path. Become a sales consultant, migrate to people management in HR or enter academia.

For the transition to go smoothly, I suggest you dedicate time (after work, weekend or during time off) to achieve the transition. Or try to gain the related skills and experiences from your current job. Once you are ready, make a move. Don't forget to define your goals and set the hard target date so that you would be on track.

This chapter went on to explain the job market and suggest job search tips that may be needed for the testing job market. The next chapter shall explore the factors that you should consider while looking for a testing role.

∧∧∧

CHAPTER 6

FACTORS TO CONSIDER FOR A TESTING ROLE

Quality is the bigger picture. Testing is a subset which as several layers and flavors to it based on the project needs. This chapter dwells on exploring some of the factors to consider while you take up a testing role.

QUALITY AND TESTING:

Quality is not only about writing Test Cases and execute Test Cases. There is a misperception between Quality Assurance and Quality Control.

Quality Control is to control the quality of the software within given or agreed processes, procedures, and activities. Normally this would focus on Testing.

On the other hand, Quality Assurance is to ensure that we would do could be able to deliver the best quality on time within budget. This is more about Software Development Project as a whole and is a higher level.

The role involves collaboration with Quality Standard, stakeholders and the team. The end goal is to ensure that we have the right process and procedure for everyone would follow (build right thing the right way).

There are many roles in which you need not write test cases, but equally important that you participate as a tester. For instance:

- Requirement understanding
- Requirement analysis
- Requirement clarification
- Ensure Lab readiness and Calibration
- Interact with suppliers
- Identifying the design bugs
- Defect reporting
- Test cases review
- Test case coverage review
- Status reporting
- Sprint planning, Backlog review, sizing the stories
- Estimation
- Ad-hoc testing
- Leading the Team
- Managing the resources
- Creating the Test Plans
- Sign off
- SPOC for QA Team
- Scrum Master
- Creating Ramp up Plan

- Knowledge Transfer
- Test Environment Setup
- Test Data Creation

AUTOMATION TESTING VERSUS MANUAL TESTING

Manual testing includes testing a software manually, i.e., without using any automated tool or any script. The tester takes over the role of an end-user and tests the software to identify any unexpected behavior. There are different levels of manual testing such as unit testing, integration testing, system testing, and user acceptance testing. Testers use test plans, test cases, or test scenarios to test the system and ensure the completeness of testing. Manual testing also includes exploratory testing, as testers explore the software to identify errors in it.

Suggested Reading: Software Testing Levels

How would you feel if you could finish the job you currently do, that takes an hour, in a couple of minutes every day without burning out?

Automation is the future because no one wants to repeat the tasks they do. Manual testing will always continue to exist but not in the same way. Look at how things have changed since the year 2000. Then compare it to the way things were in the 90s.

Automation testing, also known as Test Automation, is when the tester develops scripts or uses another software to test the product. This process involves automation of a manual process. Automation Testing is used to re-run the test scenarios that were performed manually, quickly, and repeatedly.

Apart from regression testing, automation testing is also used to test the application from load, performance, and stress point of view. It increases the test coverage, improves accuracy, and saves time and money in comparison to manual testing.

It is not possible to automate every task in a software or system. Often transactions with the user interface or any area having a large number of input combinations are worthy candidates for automation.

Furthermore, all GUI items, connections with databases, field validations, etc. can be efficiently tested by automating the manual process. The following are the basic questions to brainstorm before committing to automation:

- When to Automate?
- Why should you apply test automation?
- Project complexity
- Module Criticality
- Projects that require testing the same areas frequently
- The frequency of Requirements changes

- Accessing the application for load and performance with many virtual users
- Stable software with respect to manual testing
- Availability of time
- How to Automate?

Automation is done by using a supportive computer language like VB scripting or Python scripting and an automated software application. There are many tools available that can be used to write automation scripts.

Before mentioning the tools, let us identify the process that can be used to automate the testing process:

- Identifying areas within a software for automation
- Selection of appropriate tool for test automation
- Writing test scripts
- Development of test suits
- Execution of scripts
- Create result reports
- Identify any potential bug or performance issues

Despite automation, you still need to apply your brains to come up with valuable test ideas. Learn to communicate and describe your testing and its challenges. Be able to say exactly what you are testing for, how you will know when you have found a problem, when you will know to stop, to whom you are going to report your results, and what you are choosing not to do instead.

Bear in mind that Automation isn't the end goal, it's a way to get to the end faster. If you are limited in your testing capabilities, you can get to the wrong place faster through automation. Automation is just another tool among many tools to increase effectiveness.

This chapter went on to explain factors that you should consider while looking for a testing role and it discussed the relations between Quality and Testing and the roles you are expected to participate in as a tester. Later it also touched upon the role of automation in testing. The next chapter shall dig a little deeper to explain the basic testing concepts.

ΔΔΔ

CHAPTER 7

SOFTWARE DEVELOPMENT LIFE CYCLE, SOFTWARE TESTING LIFE CYCLE, AND BASIC TESTING TECHNIQUES

This chapter refers to some of the key testing concepts taken from the testing literature and provides you with a basic understanding of the knowledge base needed for a Software Tester. This chapter is not very extensive in theory but serves well to equip the tester with the know-how.

Software Development Life Cycle (SDLC) is a process that consists of a series of planned activities to develop or alter the Software Products. It is very important to determine what type of software development life cycle is or will be used while developing a particular system or product. Hence from a testing perspective, it is the ideal starting point to consider.

Waterfall model is most common, classic and consistent one. It clearly defines the goals and objectives of the development based on stable and strict product requirements. It is a sequential software development process. One phase can start only after the previous one was finished. So, you are to take part in the development process from its very beginning, but you can start to execute test cases only after the previous process is finished. It is also common for using an iterative waterfall model.

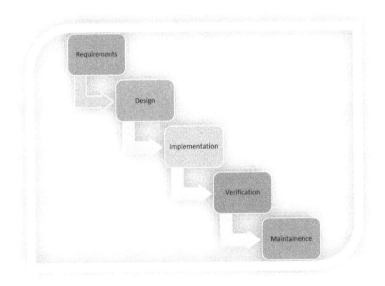

Figure 5: Waterfall Model

V model is another versatile type of SDLC. It is a very appropriate model defining the best practice of introducing testing at all levels. The diagram below illustrates that testing is done at each phase of the development cycle.

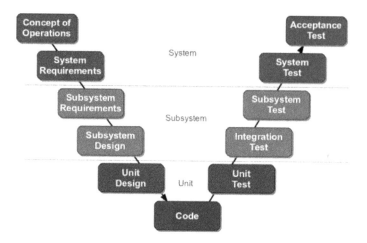

Figure 6: V Model

Agile methodology is rather flexible and dynamic. Each product is developed it its own unique way. The whole process is divided into sprints which presuppose building one particular module or one feature. A sprint consists of several parts: planning, development, testing, review, release.

But each part of the product under development is discussed and with the customer and approved beforehand. So, you can write test cases based on an approved document. The role of the tester is very important through all stages of the sprint development process because it can minimize the appearance of crashes during the release and integration of sprint.

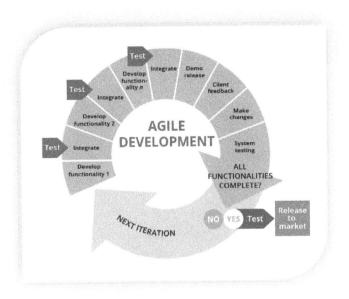

Figure 7: Agile Model

While these are the common lifecycles followed, there are other life cycle models available and are worth a read.

Suggested Reading: SDLC Tutorial

No matter what model of software development you have, the testing process, first of all, means writing test cases which takes almost a half of the whole process of testing. A well – written test case will help you on the stage of its execution and will show the adequate final result.

Whatever the SDLC considered the STLC (Software testing life cycle) is a part that should be applied in conjunction. The main activities in a testing lifecycle are as per the diagram below

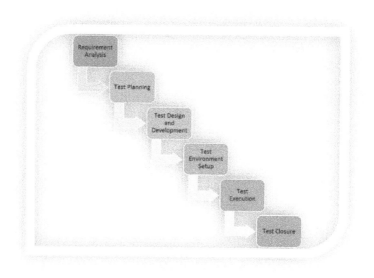

Figure 8 Software Testing Lifecycle

IT IS ALL ABOUT REQUIREMENTS

Software specifications are documents which define the functionality and technical details of a software application or system. Design Specifications can be formed after the software requirements are analyzed and solutions are chosen. Requirements state the "what" and the specs define the "how". Typically, the business segment of an organization explains their requirements and the IT (information technology) department will write the specifications to inform the software developers of the exact functionality they must implement. This is the primary reference document

- that programmers need to determine what code they must write
- in our case testers need to determine what tests they must come up with

Requirements tend to be so versatile from one project to another that it's tough to make a process on Baselining specifications.

You just need to make sure, your specifications cover everything that is asked by the business segment of the organization. As a tester, the primary role would be to identify any possible gaps and eliminate ambiguity.

Testers can make sure they flag any ambiguity with the following in mind:

- Unnecessary descriptions should be avoided.
- Coverage of all required functionalities is of absolute importance.
- Use modeling language like UML to clarify functionality.

Also, determine the testability of the given requirement. It usually falls in one of the following categories:

Inspection: Requirement can be verified by inspecting the data from a source.

Analysis: Requirement can be verified from the logs or reports the system generates.

Demonstration: Requirement can be verified via demonstrating that the system performs the intended task.

Testing: Requirement should be tested using an effective test design, if possible.

EFFECTIVE TEST DESIGN

Q: What are the inputs for creating a test case?
A: You can't write a meaningful test case without knowing the requirements. You have to know WHAT to test before HOW to test.

Test cases can't cover 100% of situations, so you should search for most probable potential weakness in a system and try to break them. Experienced testers can relate to them, but advice to relate may not be too valuable. Instead, use the classic black box testing techniques such as

- **Boundary value Analysis** - used to find the errors at boundaries of the input domain rather than finding those errors in the center of input.
- **Equivalence Partitioning** - Dividing the test input data into a range of values and selecting one input value from each range.

Example Requirement: The software controlling the incubator shall produce an audio alert when the temperature drops outside the operating range of 18°C and 56°C.

Valid Boundary Inputs (consider a resolution of 1): 18, 19, 55, 56

Invalid Boundary Inputs: 17,57

Valid Partition Inputs (consider partitioning size of 9): 18,27,36,45,54

Invalid Partition Inputs: 0,9,63

- **Decision Table Testing** – test the combinations of test conditions versus actions

Example: Consider a chart to test troubleshooting of a printer

PRINTER TROUBLESHOOTER

		Rules							
CONDITIONS	Printer prints	No	No	No	No	Yes	Yes	Yes	Yes
	A red light is flashing	Yes	Yes	No	No	Yes	Yes	No	No
	Printer is recognized by computer	No	Yes	No	Yes	No	Yes	No	Yes
ACTIONS	Check the power cable				✓				—
	Check the printer-computer cable	✓			✓				—
	Ensure printer software is installed	✓		✓		✓		✓	—
	Check/replace ink	✓	✓					✓	—
	Check for paper jam			✓		✓			—

Figure 9 Example for Decision Table Testing

- **State Transition Testing** – test the combinations for state changes

Example Requirement: The incubator door should open upon the user pressing the 'door open' button

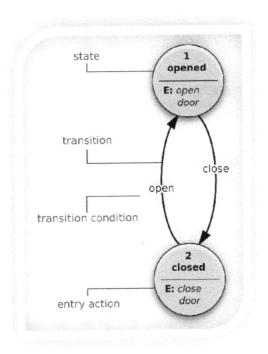

Figure 10 Example for State Transition Testing

- **Use Case Testing** – test the combination of interactions between a user and the system

Example: A user performs a banking transaction as per the use case diagram below:

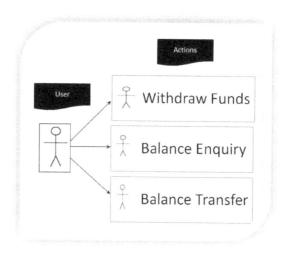

Figure 11 Example for Use Case Testing

- **Pairwise testing** - tests all the necessary parameter pairs of possible discrete combinations

Example: The software application should work on a windows environment with available OS, Processor and Database options.

Available OS list: Windows NT, Windows 8, Windows XP

Available RAM: 128MB, 512MB, 1GB

Available Processor Options: Intel Pentium, AMD, Intel Core2

Available Database options: Oracle, MySQL, Access

Test Case#	OS	RAM	Processor	Database
1	Windows NT	128MB	Intel Pentium	Oracle
2	Windows NT	512MB	AMD	MySQL
3	Windows NT	1GB	Intel Core2	Access
4	Windows 8	128MB	AMD	Access
5	Windows 8	512MB	Intel Core	Oracle
6	Windows 8	1GB	Intel Pentium	MySQL
7	Windows XP	128MB	Intel Core2	MySQL
8	Windows XP	512MB	AMD	Oracle

Figure 12 Example for Pairwise Testing

- **Negative testing** - null input, the wrong format of input, value out of normal range, wrong data type, too many values etc., can be applied in conjunction alongside unexpected environment issues (database connection failures or files corruption, for example).

If none of the above techniques fit your testing needs, you can opt for a white box testing technique that examines the following in the code.

- **Statement Coverage:** a test that each and every line of the code is executed at least once.

- **Branch Coverage:** a test that each and every branch (example: 'if' statement and its variants) of the code is executed at least once.

- **Path Coverage:** a test that all paths of the code are traversed at least once.

You can get an additional insight into what to test asking developers about details of feature implementation - they usually have thoughts about potential problems and will be happy to share them with you. But do not get biased with the development inputs. You should not be testing the software against the implementation, rather testing should be performed against the requirements. This is true at all levels of testing.

Tests should communicate their intent clearly and concisely and also map to the requirements. It is a good practice to maintain a traceability between tests and requirements to ensure adequate requirement coverage and test coverage. This is often established using a Requirement Traceability Matrix.

The significance of the test is important because when it fails, the root cause of that failure could be understood easily and quickly.

Link the input/action and the expected output to the point where there can be no question about them. Whenever this is not obvious, clarify the assumptions or preconditions that explain that link. It is pivotal to furnish all this information in the description of the test itself, whether it is described in the plain text, graphical notation, or a programming language.

Software testers are too concerned with "specifications" whereas knowing the actual business domain logic is so much more valuable than fulfilling that "specific" role. This is NOT to oversee the value of an independent tester. The overall business logic and the testing effort should complement each other.

Fundamental properties of an ideal test case:

- reproducible
- understandable - by all people who might be interested like product managers, developers, and fellow testers

- tests single set of functionalities - if the test fails, you know exactly what went wrong. This is not always practical, but it is ideal.
- can easily be tested, retested, failed, shared, communicated about
- well named and identified
- simple – possible to analyze anomalies without long investigation;
- independent - one test case shouldn't be based on the results of another;
- responsible for a focus area - different test cases shouldn't test the same features because it doesn't make sense, unobvious and requires more time for support;
- fast - running of automation tests or testing scenario manually take much time, so try to save it.
- relevance - If the test fails and no one notices or cares or wants to fix it, does the test case matter?

As far as becoming better at writing test cases, there is only one magic formula - practice. Write test cases for other people to execute. Write your own test cases and then ignore them until you don't remember the details, then go back and try to test just using what you wrote. Use test cases others wrote and edit and improve them.

Suggested Reading: *Whitepaper on Good Test Cases by Jim Kaner*

TEST CASE STRUCTURE

The general structure of the test case is as follows:

- Pre-conditions
- Test case setup
- Test case description
- Post-conditions

You should keep in mind while writing test cases that all your test cases are to be simple and easy to understand. Main test case attributes are:

- Author
- unique test ID
- title
- test case priority
- producer
- developer
- the idea of the test case
- a list of requirements mapped to the test case
- setup and additional info
- revision history
- steps to reproduce or description
- expected result
- actual result
- Result column indicating Pass/Fail
- comments
- Requirement Traceability details for each step (recommended at a test step level)

A good test case starts with a strong title. Usually, the name of the title is the same as the name of the module, feature which you are going to test. For example, if you're testing the login page, put "Login Page" as the title of the test case.

The description of the test case should contain additional information such as a test environment, test data, assumptions that apply to the test and preconditions that must be met prior to the test being executed. This information can include any special setup requirements that must be done before running the test. This information also helps to keep the test steps short and concise.

The most important part of the test case is "steps to reproduce". It is an instruction on how to observe the expected result and furnish the actual result. An effective test case must have 10-20 test steps and ideally not exceed 40 test steps. If your test case has too many steps it would be very hard to reach the result of the test considering the idea of it. In this case, it is better to separate the test case into a set of smaller ones. In case you have repeating steps in different test cases, it is better to form the repeating scenario as a separate set, and make reference to this set each time, which also will help to reduce the number of steps.

One test step covers only one expected result. That is why the expected result must be clear, precise and mapped to a requirement.

Test cases should not be connected with each other. Otherwise, if one test case is, for example, deleted or changed, the other one, which has reference to the deleted or changed test case and presupposes following its steps, will fail.

TESTING EFFORTS NEED A PLAN OF ATTACK

The test plan is a document that coordinates the process of software testing from the very beginning to all the way till the end. It describes the extent of testing operations starting from the description of the object under investigation, aims and objectives, strategies, start criteria and end criteria, tools, additional skills (training), ways of solving potential issues which may appear during the testing process.

The main aim of test plan creation is documenting of every detail of software testing in order to not waste time on different problems later. You should think of all possible risks and predict best solutions for them.

The following are the main questions a good test plan should answer:

- what is the product/system under test? - the description of the product (system) environment, features and functionalities, specifications and additional useful information.

- what should be tested? - the list of functions and the description of the testing field in general and its components in particular.
- how will the testing process be conducted? - test strategies namely: tool, methods, approaches which are to be applied.
- when should will you conduct testing? (the sequence of activities to be done: preparation, testing, and analysis of the results in the context of the planned phases of project development)
- what are start criteria? (readiness of the test platform, the degree of completion of the development if the function to be tested, availability of all required documentation)
- what are the end criteria? (the number of open issues corresponds the requirements, no new crashes appeared during the certain period of investigation, no code changes during the certain period)

Thus, the test plan includes the following:

- the description of the product (system) environment, features, and functionalities, additional useful information;
- the list of functions and the description of the testing field in general and its components in particular;
- test strategies, namely: tool, methods, test types, approaches which are to be applied;

- the sequence of activities to be done: preparation, testing, and analysis of the results in the context of the planned phases of project development;
- the readiness of the test platform, the degree of completion of the development if the function to be tested, availability of all required documentation;
- the number of open issues corresponds the requirements, no new crashes appeared during the certain period of investigation, no code changes during the certain period.

Main parts of a generic test plan are as follows:

- test plan ID, title, author
- test plan content
- Introduction (the essence of the project)
- software specification (number and title of features, priorities)
- list of features to be tested
- test approaches, methods, tools
- test documentation to be created for testing execution (test cases)
- start/end criteria
- dependencies (list of things which can influence the testing procedure: licenses, additional machines)
- software configuration to be used while testing

- circumstances under which the process of testing must be stopped/proceeded (e.g. too much crashes appeared)
- roles and responsibilities
- additional training required
- schedule (e.g. start/end date of preparation for testing and running test cases)
- risk assessment
- additional information
- approvals

This list may not be complete. Specific details may vary on the quality management system of the company, team, project specification, etc.

HUNTING DOWN BUGS AND FLUSHING THEM OUT

An unwritten rule for dealing with anomalies is "if it happens more than once, report it". Testing and bug fixing result in two key outcomes:

- Improved customer experience - the customer would buy more provide positive feedback to potential customers.
- Reduced support costs - If the customer never encounters an issue, the support team would never get pinged.

Both of them make sure a *lean methodology* is maintained and it can lead to savings in revenue.

Suggested Reading: _Lean Software Development: 7 Principles Everyone Should Follow_

An issue logged should ideally contain the following items whenever applicable:

- a detailed description of the anomaly observed.
- a screenshot or image or video or sound recording or system logs
- at which point of the application the anomaly was observed, the sequence performed before things went wrong (and how long it took after starting the application if it was recovered from sleep mode etc.).
- Steps to reproduce (if known)
- Repeatability – example: it happened 2 times in 3 days of testing.

If you have some suspicions or any other details, add them too. In general, any information, any clues which can help developers to find what caused the problem is beneficial. Also, it is much better to report the risk you can't reproduce than stay silent about it.

There are many measures to report bug severity. We typically use:

- **Critical** - this impacts the system and needs to be fixed as soon as possible
- **High** - this has a high impact, it should be included in the next update

- **Medium** - the system can be used despite the issue, include when it makes sense
- **Low** - minimal impact to most users, usually never gets addressed.

Once you do this the defect management process takes over. This is usually done by using a defect management tool.

Usually, a defect triage meeting categorizes Validity of issue is due to Software, Test Protocol, Requirements or Invalid. The development team is informed if the issue is categorized under Software implementation. The stakeholders will then choose to fix it in subsequent builds or justify not to fix. Also, an impact analysis of the defect is done to determine the amount of regression testing required.

Your role as a tester is to perform regression testing and verify that the issue is fixed without affecting the other modules in the system.

This chapter went on to explore the key theories in the literature behind software testing. Starting with the common Software development Life Cycles followed by the various steps Software testing Lifecycle namely Requirement Analysis, Test Design and development, Test planning, Test Execution, Test Reporting and Defect Management. The next chapter shall present the case for implementing tools using which the Software Testing Lifecycle can be simplified and better managed. We shall also explore some of the test automation tools.

ΔΔΔ

CHAPTER 8

TEST MANAGEMENT TOOLS AND AUTOMATION TOOLS

The testing life cycle may get cumbersome in handling the processes and volume of documentation depending on the size and complexity of the testing project. This chapter explores few of the options available to you as a tester to perform your task efficiently using the right tool.

Historically manual testing was documented using pen and paper. Some highly regulated projects follow this trend even now. But maintaining electronic copies are simpler, lean, cost-effective and environment-friendly. Manual testing is time-consuming, expensive, especially with iterative development. You can save a lot of time by automating parts of the process, as discussed in the previous chapter. Hence it would be beneficial to use suitable tools for supporting all stages of the testing process.

You can execute manual tests in various ways such as pen and paper, spreadsheets, mobile apps, or using more integrated application management solutions such as HP ALM. An opensource ALM solution such as SpiraTest, TestRail, etc. may be more affordable and easier to use. The advantage of using a tool is that you have a single place for your test cases, user stories, results and defects that allow easier communication between testers, developers, and managers.

Free Open source Test Case Management Tools:

- Tarantula
- Testopia
- qaManager
- TestLink
- Kiwi TCMS
- TestMaster
- WebTst
- Salome-TMF

Most of the Test management tools also can be integrated with Automation Tools. Automation testing can be useful to perform repetitive testing tasks. In my recent interview with the life sciences division of Google, I learned that they are very keen on using automation as much as possible to prevent tester errors and making the test cycle faster. They invest a lot in automation tools. In my experience, UI elements and logging are candidates for exploring automation. However, automation may get complicated in testing core-algorithmic requirements in a product.

The following tools can be used for automation testing:

- HP Quick Test Professional – web applications
- Selenium – web applications
- Appium – mobile applications
- See-test – mobile applications
- Swish – UI elements
- Cucumber – other software applications
- Katalon Studio
- TestComplete
- WinRunner
- LoadRunner – Nonfunctional/Performance
- LabVIEW – Simulation Models
- WATIR - Web Application Testing in Ruby.

Industry experts argue that automation testing is taking over manual testing in projects. Many organizations approach automation testing to be a valuable addition. This is particularly relevant with PC, mobile, and web-based applications and is open for consideration for UI and multilingual testing in embedded devices.

An ideal starting point for test automation would be using record and playback testing tools such as Selenium followed by learning to use a scripting language to create a test. An example would be using Python or Perl scripting.

Suggested Reading:
- _Comparison of automated testing tools_

- *Testing with Python: Just makes sense*

Agile is the new sought Lifecycle - lots of companies are transitioning from traditional waterfall methods to agile development. This is due to the simplicity, lower cost and the quicker tuned round time. So the demand for agile testing is growing.

Lastly, clients have a Focus on business value - Testing efforts are directed towards those risks that can cost money, business-wise. An example would be earlier involvement in the development process. Instead of waiting until the product is almost finished, testers are getting involved earlier in the process, when the requirements are defined.

This chapter went on to explore the software testing tools and test automation tools that can make life easier for test management. The next chapter explores the recent trends and focus areas were testing needs a new heading and adaptation.

ΛΛΛ

CHAPTER 9

RECENT TRENDS

With the advancement in technology and smart services, testing has also become a field for value addition. The mainframes and computing assets of a company have changed drastically over a decade. Cloud Infrastructure, IOT, and machine learning applications are taking over traditional mundane tasks.

It is very important for the modern tester to stay relevant in the current industry. This chapter dwells upon such key areas.

API TESTING

More and more apps are being developed lately. Development activities are transforming towards API's (Application Programming Interface) from Web-based. Also, the web is increasingly becoming a device independent and platform independent space. Business requirements often demand a seamless experience over PC and mobile environments. A low hanging fruit for most businesses would be to make their web experience the same over a variety of devices, browsers, and operating systems. Also, there is a debate about having a native app versus a mobile web-based application.

API's are the next big thing since they provide the following features:

- **Control**—Create and update interfaces on your own time schedule, rather than waiting for your product vendors.
- **Flexibility**—If you decide you should share more or less data, you can quickly make those changes.
- **Value**—You pay one flat fee for the API console developers, and you can create as many interfaces as you want, with whatever agencies or programs you want.

Hence new trends are slowly shifting to towards providing ERROR free interoperable, adaptable and scalable API model to enterprises.

API testing thus translates into the following:

Reduced overheads

API testing comes along with component/integration levels. Hence enables to discover critical interface bugs at very early stages.

Discover Interface errors

The interface is a common boundary between two separate systems. Since API's communicate between to separate components, interface errors are highlighted in API testing

Reducing build failures

API testing can be considered as a structural test approach intended to test the structure or flow of a program.

Enhanced functional testing without GUI

Functional features available for testing without the need of GUI.

MOBILITY

Figure 13 Mobility

Companies are thinking twice about taking mobile app development as a lower priority. As per user study statistics, more searches are made on mobile devices than on a desktop. Hence companies are compelled to hop on the mobile bandwagon or be left behind by their competitors. As a matter of fact, it is not just enough to desire mobile, these days, it has to be mobile first, as evidenced by bigwigs in the tech sector. Google, in particular, are providing tools and platforms to support the growth of different apps on mobile devices. This new mobile-first focus has spurred innovation in functionality and user experience.

Suggested Reading: *Mobile Testing Tutorial*

BLOCKCHAIN TECHNOLOGY

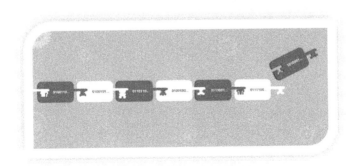

Figure 14 Blockchain

Perhaps Blockchain is arguably the hottest topic in technology today. While blockchain is also associated with cryptocurrency it is not the only field of use. It should be noted that blockchain technology can be integrated with virtually any application, owing to its encryption and data integrity features. Not only is the irreversible ledger being used to facilitate mobile payments via apps like Fold and BitPay, it is also being used in the logistics and retail businesses to improve efficiency. There are many examples of blockchain-dependent apps on the market today, with the number of apps and businesses looking to leverage on the many benefits of blockchain technology only set to increase in the years to come. Security and integrity of these blockchains would be good candidates for testing.

Suggested Reading: *A Beginner's Guide to Testing Blockchain Applications*

THE INTERNET OF THINGS (IOT)

Figure 15 IoT

'Smart' is not only associated with mobile phones these days, now, we have smart houses, smart devices, smart lighting, and even smart cities. This is made possible, in part, by sensors embedded in these devices, which make automation, monitoring, and remote control possible. However, these devices cannot run on their own, as they are usually controlled via the internet using the browser or smartphone apps. This presents app development companies and savvy entrepreneurs with myriad opportunities to jump into a booming industry – particularly when it comes to consumer products. In fact, a report by Business Insider notes that the smart home devices industry will more than double by 2020. Hence testing these IoT applications is expected to stay highly relevant.

Suggested Reading: _IoT testing: How to overcome 5 big challenges_

AUGMENTED REALITY

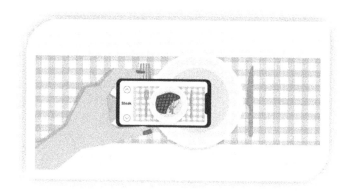

Figure 16 Augmented Reality

The potential uses and benefits of Augmented Reality (AR) for businesses are innumerable even though it is not a recent mobile app development trend. This potential is not limited solely to consumers, but for in-house benefits too, such as for training purposes. For example, businesses can visualize how their products and services work in real-time and explain their benefits to potential customers. A practical example of this is how the IKEA Place allows users to see how furniture fits into their space, with AR making it possible for them to choose the best fit for furniture from the comfort of their homes. That said, the use of AR is not limited to just businesses, but extends to virtually all other niches like games, food, and education. For example, Kabaq helps users visualize how a restaurant's food will look on your table, while Quiver brings children's art and drawings to life and Google uses AI and AR more than ever before. There are a lot of algorithms in the background whose logic needs to be sound and there lies the opportunity for testing.

Suggested Reading: _5 ways AI will change software testing_

WEARABLE DEVICE APPS

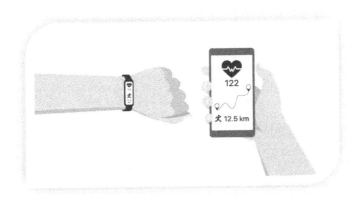

Figure 17 Wearable devices, Mobile and Apps

The growth of wearable device apps is another notable mobile app development trend to look out for in 2018. The wearable device market is expected to grow to $223.3 million by 2021 according to reports by International Data Corporation (IDC). While the market is dominated by wristbands like Fitbit, the niche for other wearable devices, such as smartwatches, is gaining traction. Even though some of these devices have their own features, their capabilities are expanded through support from smartphones, which require apps. Another major factor in wearable devices gaining traction is that, aside from their functionalities, they have more or less also become fashion accessories. This is definitely a market worth pursuing hence the relevant for testing avenues.

Suggested Reading: *Testing In The Land Of Wearables: Taming The Wild, Wild West*

ANDROID INSTANT APPS

Figure 18 Android Instant Apps

Android Instant Apps is set to be a regular feature of current practices and future trends in app development. As the name implies, Android Instant Apps allow users to enjoy apps without having to install them locally on their devices. That is, users can see an app in the Google Play Store and decide to give it a try without downloading it. There are many upsides to this – first, an Android app development company can make it easy for users to try the app, thus, increasing the chances of success as these apps are also easy to share. From the users' perspective, however, major benefits include being able to use instant apps from anywhere while not having to worry about their device's storage memory. With these benefits, it's easy to see why we are predicting that Instant Apps will be flooding the Play Store.

Suggested Reading: *How to test Android Instant Apps?*

LAZY LOADING (DYNAMIC FUNCTION LOADING) AND ACCELERATED MOBILE PAGES (AMP)

Figure 19 Dynamic Function Loading and AMP

Google, in tandem with other tech companies such as Twitter, created what is now known as Accelerated Mobile Pages. The project is a recognition of the need to create web pages that are "consistently fast, beautiful, and high-performing across devices and distribution platforms." On the other hand, lazy loading ensures that users get to view the webpage even while some assets or components of the website have yet to be loaded. These two features are specifically important for apps whose content is syndicated through content on web pages. This would, of course, reduce the application start-up time as well as limit memory usage. Performance testing is an area of focus for such applications.

EASIER LOGINS AND INCREASED SECURITY

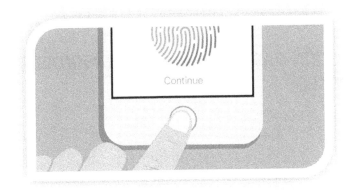

Figure 20 Secured Authentication

While passwords aren't going anywhere anytime soon, one can argue that users are somewhat inundated with the many passwords they have to keep up with. It is for this reason that apps are increasingly incorporating biometric identification and authentication as a means of verification. This, coupled with the increasing number of confidential and sophisticated data exchanges on smartphones these days, proves that the need for increased security has never been this pronounced. Therefore, there's no denying that web design and development companies need to embed security features into the apps they build. There are already devices with touch ID and facial recognition, and we predict more companies will use these in their app development. There's also a case for other security and login mechanisms such as verification codes and two-factor authentication. Security Testing is paramount in such applications.

LOCATION-BASED AND PERSONALIZED SERVICES

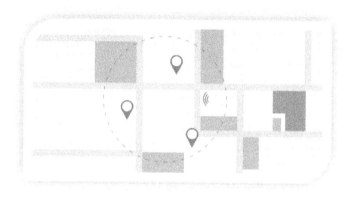

Figure 24 Location-based services

In the grand scheme of things, mobile apps are marketing tools in and of themselves. For this reason, marketers require content tailored to the specific needs of the user. Even for standalone applications, there are instances where personalized content works well for the user's experience. This is made possible by geofencing and location-based services. A simple example of this would be a weather app that gives users different notifications on the weather based on where they are. However, more recently, the use of Bluetooth beacons is on the rise; Apple's iBeacon and

Google beacon come to mind in this regard. In 2018, these technologies will definitely be part of the top trends in mobile app development. Localization tests, location-based real-time tests, and range-based tests are very relevant in these scenarios.

MOBILE PAYMENTS

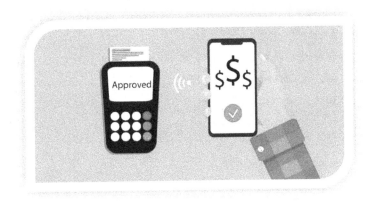

Figure 22 Mobile payments

According to a report by IT Pro Portal, by 2020, 90% of smartphone owners will have made at least one form of mobile payment. The truth is, mobile payments are convenient and perhaps the fastest mode of payment, and their adoption is growing apace as shown by the aforementioned forecast. Platforms such as Apple Pay and Google Wallet offer smartphone users great potential, especially for e-commerce transactions. So great is the potential of mobile payments that Android Pay and Google Wallet have merged into a single platform called Google Pay, as introduced by Google during CES 2018. Google Pay is already associated with apps like Airbnb, Instacart, and others. Suffice to say that e-commerce website development, and by extension, any apps wherein money is exchanged, need to integrate mobile payments.

2018 will be the year of the latest mobile app development trends listed above. They will be implemented on a large scale – some, larger than they've ever been. If you're looking to validate such systems, be sure that the apps conform to safety in everchanging the app market.

Suggested Reading: *Testing 101 for Digital Payments*

ROBOTICS

Robotics has been around for a long time and it did not take much effort for mega services to recognize its value. In 2015, Uber began the trend by hitting its autonomous car on the roads of Pittsburgh. Now, its Tesla, BMW, and many major services that are all set to begin the robust journey of robotics. Not only on roads, but robotics will also dominate over the healthcare sectors in the form of wheelchairs, nurses, etc.

To keep the system running, software testing teams need to get strictly geared up because robotics is going to be a tough challenge in the years to come. Take a glimpse into the future and you will see Robot-as-a-Service rising, more incentives for the experts, the Governments becoming an investor, and much more

While software-based robots will be programmed by Cloud that would allow decentralization and control access to other linked robots as well. Hence, it is totally clear that the future is about all whopper IT things and software testers should know what their next new topic should be to learn.

Suggested Reading: *Robotics: The future of testing*

BIG DATA

Here's an example for you, in the coming year, even your car's tire will become integrated with sensors that will wirelessly connect with the telemetry boxes and cloud serving as a big data resource for you.

Now you would have known that how Big Data combined with IoT and AI going to turn the IT world totally wireless and connected.

Big Data is going to be tech-lit as it will see quite rigorous innovations and recreations such as perspective analysis, Dark Data, Machine Learning, and intensified cybersecurity tends.

Due to the volume of data processed testing Big Data application would be a new challenge.

Considering the concepts and focus areas explained in this chapter, you the tester can enhance your knowledge from even more testing literature and know-hows by exploring the testing resources listed in the final chapter. It is highly recommended that you go through the links in the order of preference that is most relevant to you.

Suggested Reading: *The Big Data Testing Challenges You Should Know About*

ΛΛΛ

CHAPTER 10

TESTING RESOURCES

This chapter contains a collection of useful testing resources handpicked by a community of testers. This will take you a long way on the journey to a Subject Matter Expert.

Most of the links are free to use open source contributions. Please explore the following links and prioritize the concepts that are most relevant to you.

SOFTWARE TESTING THEORY

- Perspectives on Agile Software Testing – Thought Works
- A Practical Guide to Testing in DevOps – Katrina Clokie
- Programs and Proofs. Mechanizing Mathematics with Dependent Types. – Ilya Sergey
- Measure Software Quality using Application Security – Dinis Cruz
- The "A" Word – Alan Page
- Acceptance Test Engineering Guide, Vol. I – Grigori Melnik, Gerard Meszaros

- A Software Testing Primer (PDF) – Nick Jenkins
- Classic Testing Mistakes (PDF) – Brian Marick
- Code Coverage Analysis – Steve Cornett
- Practical Software Testing – STH in association with Chindam Damodar
- A Tutorial in Exploratory Testing (PDF) – Cem Kaner
- Essential Acceptance Testing – Toby Weston
- Embedded Software Testing Methods – Juho Lepistö
- Foundations of Software Testing: Fundamental Algorithms and Techniques –Aditya P. Mathur
- Introduction to software testing (PDF) – Paul Ammann, Jeff Offutt
- Manual Testing Help – *Software Testing Help* Website
- Performance Testing Guidance – J.D Meier et al.
- Software Testing: A Comprehensive Approach – Bill Laboon
- Software Testing Tutorial – *Tutorials point* Website
- Software Testing Dictionary – *Tutorials point* Website
- The Way of Testivus – Alberto Savoia
- The Little Black Book on Test Design (PDF) – Rikard Edgren

- The Essential Guide to Mobile App Testing (PDF) – Utest
- Handbook of Software Reliability Engineering – Michael R. Lyu
- Mutation Testing: Better Code by Making Bugs – Filip van Laenen
- The Tao of Testing. A Field Manual for Software Engineers – Jason Polites
- Observing and Reasoning About Errors – Jerry Weinberg

STANDARDS IN SOFTWARE TESTING

- Testing Standards Working Party
- The International Software Testing Standard
- The standard for Software Component Testing (PDF)
- Everything You Need to Know About Software Test Formats (page is in Russian so please use google translate)
- Software Testing Standards in NASA
- ECSS-Q-ST-80C Rev.1 – Software product assurance

TESTING OF FREE AND OPENSOURCE SOFTWARE

- Quality Improvement in Volunteer Free and Open Source Software Project (PDF) - Martin Michlmayr

TESTING USING DIFFERENT PROGRAMMING LANGUAGES

- PHPUnit PHP Test-Driven Development – Automated Tools to Improve Your PHP Code Quality – *DZone* website
- Practical PHP testing – Giorgio Sironi
- Testing Erlang
- Testing in Scala
- Test-Driven Development – Extensive Tutorial – Grzegorz Gałęzowski
- Testing and Debugging JavaScript
- Web Application Testing in Ruby - Željko Filipin

TESTING TOOL TUTORIALS

- The Evolving Art of Fuzzing (PDF) – Jared DeMott
- AccelTest (PDF)
- A Step-by-Step Guide to Functional Testing with TestComplete – *Smart Bear* Website

- HP Quality Center Tutorial – *Tutorials point* Website
- HP QuickTest Professional Tutorial – *Tutorials point* Website
- .NET Performance Testing and Optimization – The Complete Guide (zip) – RedGate, By Paul Glavich and Chris Farrell
- Record-Playback Test Automation: Sahi & Selenium IDE – Shashikant Jagtap
- Selenium 2.0 Using the WebDriver API to Create Robust User Acceptance Tests – Matt Stine
- SoapUI 101: Beginner's Guide to Functional Testing – *Smart Bear* Website
- TestNG Tutorial – *Tutorials point* Website
- Junit Tutorial– *Tutorials point* Website
- PropEr Testing – Fred Hebert
- Better Unit Testing with Microsoft Fakes – *Microsoft* Website
- Testing for Continuous Delivery with Visual Studio 2012 – *Microsoft* Website

FORMAL METHODS

- Learn TLA+ - Hillel Wayne
- Specifying Systems – Leslie Lamport
- The TLA+ Hyperbook – Leslie Lamport

- Books and papers about TLA+ and formal verification – Leslie Lamport
- Introduction to Spin – Multiple Authors
- Software Foundations – Benjamin C. Pierce & Co
- Verified Functional Algorithms – Andrew W. Appel
- Foundations of Computer Science – Dr. Larry Paulson
- Principles of Model Checking – Christel Baier, Joost-Pieter Katoen
- Certified Programming with Dependent Types – Adam Chlipala
- Formal Reasoning About Programs – Adam Chlipala
- Concrete Semantics – Tobias Nipkow and Gerwin Klein
- ML for the Working Programmer, 2nd Edition – Lawrence C. Paulson
- Proofs and Types – Jean-Yves Girard, Yves Lafont, and Paul Taylor
- Proof assistants: History, ideas, and future – H. Geuvers
- Design and validation of computer protocols – Gerard J. Holzmann
- Introduction to Logic – Michael Genesereth, Eric Kao (Stanford University)

- <u>An Introduction to Formal Logic</u> – P.D. Magnus (University at Albany)
- <u>A Problem Course in Mathematical Logic</u> – Stefan Bilaniuk (Trent University)
- <u>Language, Proof, and Logic</u> – Jon Barwise, John Etchemendy
- <u>Mathematical Logic</u> – Helmut Schwichtenberg
- <u>Mathematical Logic</u> – Stephen G. Simpson (Pennsylvania State University)
- <u>Formal Logic</u> – Miguel Palomino
- <u>Is Parallel Programming Hard, And, If So, What Can You Do About It?</u> (chapters "Validation" and "Formal verification") – Paul E. McKenney
- <u>Formal Methods of Software Design</u> – Eric Hehner

MOOC AND OPEN LEARNING

You can audit most of the below-mentioned testing courses for free. However, the MOOC provider may charge for a verified certificate.

- <u>Software Testing</u> (Platform: Udacity)

- <u>Software Testing Fundamentals</u> (the University of Maryland, Platform: edX)

- <u>Software Testing Management</u> (the University of Maryland, Platform: edX)

- <u>Software Engineering Essentials</u> (Technische Universität München, Platform: edX)

- <u>Testing with Agile</u> (the University of Virginia, Platform: Coursera)

- <u>Learning test-driven development in Java</u> (Platform: Udemy)

- <u>Selenium WebDriver training with Java Basics</u> (Platform: Udemy)

- <u>Introduction to Software Testing</u> (Platform: Alison)

- <u>Software Testing – Testing Levels and Object-Oriented Program Testing</u> (Platform: Alison)

- <u>Software Testing – Black-Box Strategies and White-Box Testing</u> (Platform: Alison)

- <u>Software Testing – Condition Coverage and Mutation Testing Strategies</u> (Platform: Alison)

ΔΔΔ

CONCLUDING REMARKS

I hope this book has provided you with the fundamental know-how for a prospective tester. This book is just a stepping stone to further learning, never an encyclopedia for testing. I have tried to cover the most essential elements for someone who is new to the testing field. I have tried to balance theory and experience effectively to get to the point.

I hope you have enjoyed reading the book. Do let me know your feedback and reviews. If you have any ideas or clarifications you are more than welcome to reach out!

Do check out my other books through my publication blog at http://about.me/kvna

∆∆∆

ACRONYMS AND ABBREVIATIONS

Abbreviations	Definition
AI	Artificial Intelligence
AMP	Accelerated Mobile Pages
API	Application Programming Interface
AR	Augmented Reality
BE	Bachelors in Engineering
BITS	Birla Institute of Technology and Science
B-school	Business School

Abbreviations	*Definition*
CAPA	Corrective Action and Preventive Action
CES	Consumer Electronics Show
CMMi	Capability Maturity Model Integration
COPQ	Cost of Poor Quality
CV	Curriculum Vitae
DOORS	Dynamic Object-Oriented Requirements System
DRE	Defect Removal Efficiency
ERP	Enterprise resource planning
FAA	Federal Aviation Administration

Abbreviations	Definition
FDA	Food and Drug Administration
FT	Financial Times
GDP	Good Documentation Practices
GMP	Good Manufacturing Practices
GUI	Graphical User Interface
HP ALM	Application Lifecycle Management by Hewlett Packard
ID	Identification
IDC	International Data Corporation
IOT	Internet of Things

Abbreviations	*Definition*
IT	Information Technology
MBA	Masters of Business Administration
MIS	Management Information Systems
MS	Master of Science
QA	Quality Assurance
QMS	Quality Management System
QTP	Quick Test Pro
SDLC	Software Development Life Cycle
SPOC	Specific Point of Contact
SQA	Software Quality Assurance

Abbreviations	Definition
SQL	Structured Query Language
STEM	Science, Technology, Engineering, and Math
STLC	Software Testing Lifecycle
SVP	Senior Vice-President
TcoE	Testing Centers of Excellence
UI	User Interface
UML	Unified Modeling Language
US	United States of America
V&V	Verification and Validation
VB	Visual Basic
VP	Vice-President

Abbreviations	Definition
WATIR	Web Application Testing in Ruby

www.ingramcontent.com/pod-product-compliance
Lightning Source LLC
Chambersburg PA
CBHW031244050326
40690CB00007B/939